Till Death Do Us Part

written by

INONDA C. PETERSON

TILL DEATH DO US PART

Cover Design and Illustrations by: Jyotsna Gyanani

Layout Design by: Rein G.

To all of my siblings,
may you all experience true love
and never be scared to trust again.

ACKNOWLEDGEMENTS

I sincerely thank all my family and friends
who instilled in me the confidence to turn my dreams
into reality.
Life is a crazy roller coaster,
and the ones who choose to walk alongside us
through thick and thin are to be honored.
I especially thank my Aunt Mathilda
who never let her belief in me waver.
There were times she believed in me more than
I believed in myself.
Most of all, I give glory to Jesus for breathing life
into me when my thoughts overpowered my will to live,
giving me a chance to turn my dreadful pain into purpose,
and the ability to express my scornful feelings in words
so that I can impact those across the world!

The Birth of Till Death Do Us Part

I began writing at fifteen, keeping my work hidden away, fearful of revealing my vulnerability. At eighteen, I experienced heartbreak and realized my words were more than just expressions – they were poetry, capturing the essence of my emotions and experiences. I started focusing on love, a theme that deeply resonated with me and my peers. During this period, *Till Death Do Us Part* was conceived, born from heartbreak and countless tears, each word penned through the silent sobs that escaped my lips.

The pencil glided across the pages, accompanied only by tears. In secret, I was engulfed in despair, unreachable even to those closest to me. I bottled up my feelings, hiding my tears behind a smile. Vulnerability felt like a weakness, hardening my heart and eroding my sensitivity to others. Hurt people hurt people, and the accumulated pain within me finally caused me to fracture.

Through poetry, I found a way to channel my emotions and begin the healing process. *Till Death Do Us Part* stands as a testament to my journey serving as a constant reminder that even in our darkest moments, there is a way to find light and start anew.

I am thrilled to release my poetry collection at nineteen. I hope it serves as a source of healing and a powerful reminder to teenagers everywhere that their emotions are valid and profound.

THE HEART TABS

Perfect Love

To have and to hold – Us

Till Death Do Us Part
   i will shout
         And scream!
Until my vocal cords can no longer contain
The words i have to say!

   But until then, the whole world will hear
         How in love i am with You
            Boy!

As the ground shakes beneath me
And the snakes and worms
   Scram for new coverage
   From my passionate stomps
That are stomping to the beat
   Of my own drums!

Till Death Do Us Part
We whispered
As Your eyes draw
my lips closer
         And closer
Man,
i am so in love with You
      Boy!

how me?

it was the love You saw in me
that made me believe
that i could be loved
by someone like You.

when i look into Your pretty eyes,
i see all of me –
the bad and the good,
but You still love me.

how can You love a girl like me?

do You love me?

"Yes, I do!"

am i still pretty to You?

"As pretty as ever!"

why do You like me?

"Because you, are you!"

i don't understand how You can love a girl like me.

my hair doesn't flow nearly as long as the girls on TV,
    my face is covered with bumps and blemishes
that the whole world can see,
    my body isn't nearly as curvy
as the girls You like on IG,
    my smile isn't nearly as bright
and i am not the view that everyone wants to see.

You found a beauty in me
that i don't think anyone else will see.

    so how can You love a girl like me?

sweet melodies

i lose all sense of time
as Your hands
make their way toward my waist
   grabbing me
   with no restraints on where they may go

i gravitate towards
 the safe place i found in between Your arms
   all doubt begins to roll off of me
as the pain of life
becomes a figment of my imagination
in Your presence

Your eyes scan the physique
that God has given me
marking that i am all Yours

You pull me closer as
   You whisper to my ears
   sweet melodies
that make all my insecurities vanish
sweet melodies

that i want to hear
 again
        and
            again
as if the more You say it
the more You mean it
the more i will believe it.

perfect match

a puzzle piece You were
that slipped between the cracks
a part of me
  was far gone
out of sight
but not out of mind
  then suddenly
      You strolled along
      like the stars
        complete the night
          You were the half
              that completed my life.

a million stars could not compare
to the flame You lit inside of me.

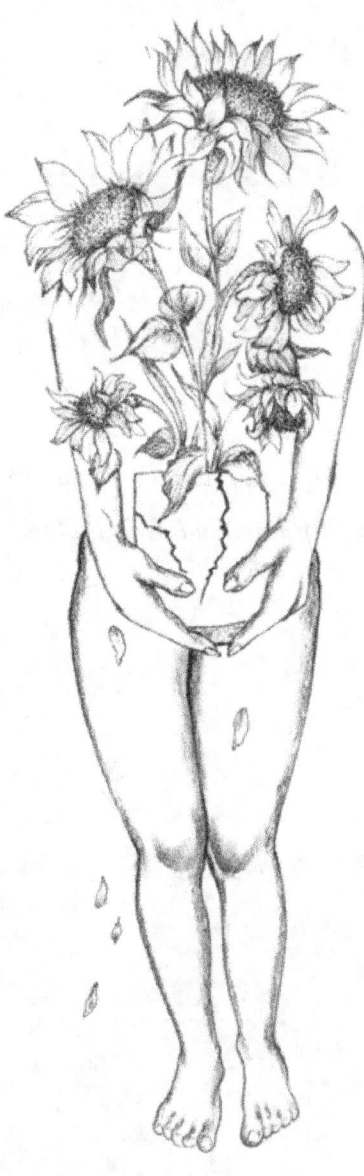

The Shift

sudden change

i see hesitation dripping off of You
while You desperately try to push the
words through the doors of Your mouth.

a slight stutter ties Your tongue.

i repeat,
all i see is You,
but am i all You see?

You prance around the question
while the eyes that once called me home
are now pushing me away.
"I just want to be alone, apart from you,"
You exclaim.

is this where the story of Us ends?

where my name,
no longer tastes of sweet satisfaction fulfilling all Your cravings?

where my touch,
no longer calms You from the anxieties of life?

where my kiss,
no longer soothes Your worries away?

where Your heart,
no longer drenches itself in sorrow
when apart from mine?

Nothing more, Nothing less

the connection
that we shared
washed away the lovers of my past
who could compare
to the one i adore?
i say!

covered in dust
and rags
You were the collector
that saw the beauty
in all my ashes

i was a work of art
uncovered by You
left for Your eyes to
gaze upon

Your fingers traced every
line
    curve
       and
          shape
outlining every imperfection
as if they were perfection

You admired me in a way
  that i have not been
touched me in a way
  that i have not felt

but as time went on
  dust began to collect
covering the beauty
that You once uncovered

i guess after a while the same
        lines
            curves
              and
                   shapes
become nothing more
than brush strokes on a canvas
that can easily be
replaced.

fading

while my love for You grew deeper and more intense,
the love You had for me began to fade
unknowingly.

as i undressed myself and walked into my most vulnerable state,
i gave You my heart and said,
here, take it.

as i made my secrets known to You,
You began to cover Yours.

who would have known Your love was fading
as You repeated the words,
"I love you,"
    day by day,
        night by night.

as Your love drifted
    further
       and
          further away,
i lost the place i had in Your heart
unknowingly.
forgotten in Your heart,
    Your love emerged in mine.
              gone but not forgotten
                 my heart whispered...

i squeezed You with a tightness
that screamed please don't let me go.

Her?

why?

in the blink of an eye, You and i were no longer
You moved on so quickly
that i had to keep my goodbyes

i assured myself it wasn't because of me You left
but i could only convince myself so much

i was nothing more than a piece of gum to You
You chewed me up
            swished me around
                        and then spit me out
when i was no longer flavorful to You

You popped in another one
with no care or concern
            of where i went

            You disposed me
                        leaving me to dry
                                    and harden.

replaced

it wasn't just the absence of You
that destroyed every last nerve
causing my vision to burn
with fury

bloodshot eyes
and You're the reason
    scratches
        and scrapes
You were the addiction
that numbed my sorrow

now You're the affliction
    that suffocates me
in silence

a substitution
in place of Your absence
what's Your
substitute for me?

i know it's more bearable
   than mine
but it's the only way i can
feel alive

  is that how She makes You feel?
    like Your head is above water?
      was She the lottery that was won?

    why did She catch Your attention
in place of me?
is She enough
       for You?

despite me

it was the knowing
    that i wasn't enough

and all my efforts to make
You feel special
were in vain

i would say
She is only half of me
but how can i?

when She is the one
in place of me

She is the one
    greeting You with kisses

  She is the one
      looking
    for You in the crowds

She is the one

        making You laugh

She is the one

        tracing

    the heart-shaped mole

      behind

        Your ear

not i

not me

no longer.

it was Her.

was She the reason
You no longer found time
in Your busy schedule
 just to call
 just to text
just to make sure i was all right?

 was She the reason why
our conversations
no longer lasted until
 the crack of dawn?

was She the reason why
i dug for
topics to talk about?

was She the reason why
 we could no longer
  sit in silence
 without You leaving?

was She the reason why
Your likes and comments
   no longer flooded my posts?
and pictures of me
no longer flooded Your story?

it was Her,
She was the reason.

She was enough
     for You.

it was Her,
    that You needed
    that You wanted

  not me,
but why not me?

my mind expected Her
but my heart wished it was always just me.

did You forget?

two worlds collide

a familiar stranger
i call You

while we bury our heads in our phones
as we walk past each other

like our two worlds never collided
leaving collateral damage to mine

You
knowing all of me
and me
knowing all of You
Your desires
        Your wants
and the fears that kept You up all night

how could i forget?
when the memories of Us
were the lullabies
that laid me to rest

now a moment in history
that seems to not exist

as if it were removed from the timeline
and only me and You know

but it was You who removed our history
like our timeline didn't matter
and the effects that were caused didn't affect You

like we were on two different sides of history

i'm black
    and You're white

i'm damaged
    and You're not

i'm hopeless
    and You're hopeful

and You're thriving
    while i'm falling into a pit
        where i see no exit

nothing to brace my fall
i might just hit rock bottom.

made alive

do You ever reminisce
  about the way
Your hands once pursued my body?

        the way Your lips once
                pushed against my skin
                    leaving marks of passion
that only Your eyes could see?
        and Your hands could touch?

marks that told the story of
        our intense love
that left no room for confusion
because i knew You were
  who i wanted
  who i needed
to survive the strike of my loneliness

live

   love

      and

          laugh

that phrase became alive

in Your presence

now in Your absence

if You ask me what those words mean

i would say they mean

nothing

without

You.

my world

the only time
i visit You is in my dreams
or when my mind scrambles
through the memories of Us
when i am occupied with the things of
life.

but i guess You
were my world
the one who sustained my
life.

now You're the one who deprives
me of the joys of
life.

we once were inseparable
now distance has separated Us
not just physically but mentally
i am deprived.

now You walk away
with half of me
i guess it's true
hearts don't break
evenly.

You caught amnesia
while i drowned in the memories
of Us.

after the departure

washed away

i looked for perfection in those i laid eyes on
it seemed as if love led me astray
and embodied me with grief and distrust

imperfect people dwelling in an imperfect world
trying to give each other a Perfect Love
an unforgettable and everlasting love
that more times than not ends with disaster

expecting nothing less than perfection
where realization quickly takes me back
to the reality of not receiving the same love i give out
by the time realization hits it's too late

i gave You the keys to my soul
and said,
here, do as You please
while hoping You would be diligent enough
to treat my heart with the same care as i would

i thought i was freeing myself by giving all of me to You
but You locked my mind in a cage that only ever thinks about You

free me,
free me,

i gave You the keys

although i let You in
You didn't stay
like the tides of the ocean
You were here one minute
gone the next
while washing away parts of me
that You promised to keep safe

as the tide came back in
and washed everything to the shore
i slowly found parts of me that were unrecognizable

damaged
and
picked apart
to something less than what it was

my identity
my trust
my dignity
are now brittle

who am i?

who am i?

i wander the open plains of my heart and mind,
searching for answers,
answers that will bring me peace.

my heart and mind are inflamed,
as i search for answers that will cool me down.

who am i truly?

am i the person i reveal to the outside world?
or am i the person i conceal deep down,
the one in constant pursuit of an escape
through my heart,
through the creases of my lips,
waiting for a chance to be heard,
to be loved?

my deepest and darkest thoughts –
                        is that *who I am?*
   is she who makes me, me?

or am i who my friends perceive me to be?

or am I all the negative

doubts,

regrets,

and

insecurities

i hide deep down in the darkest parts of my mind,
too shy to show the world all my downfalls?
who am i?
is the question.

i dream of the person i want to be
as i run away from the person i am every day.
as i run away from my thoughts,
i look for a quiet place,
but i find no peace.

i cannot escape me nor can i escape the truth,

but what is my truth?

who am i?

are my thoughts my own,

or are they all the outside voices creeping in

telling me

who i am?

                                     I am the little voice in my head

that is being crushed by the outside,

fighting for a chance

to be loved, to be heard,

the little voice that is fighting for the love of my own heart –

who am i?

You picked me apart, exposing parts of me
without reason, without regard.

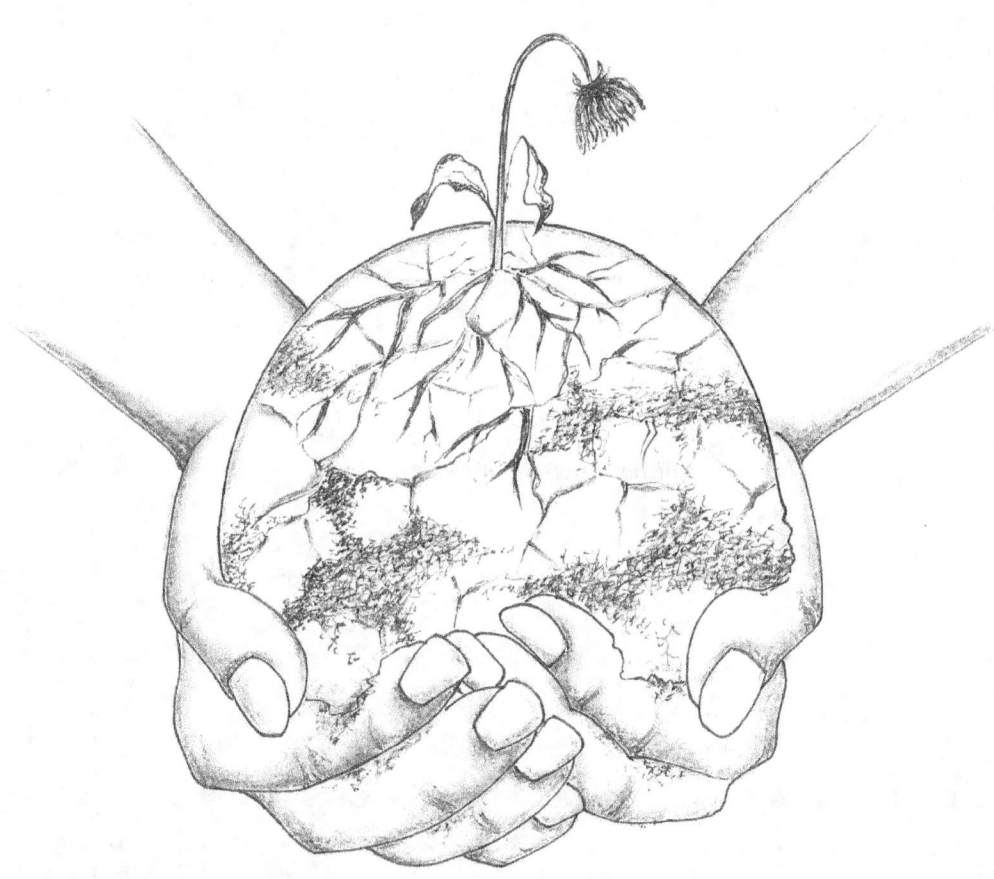

a
world without You

not You

i reluctantly hand myself over into his arms.
every inch of my body tenses and
jerks from his touch –

i begin to lose the sensitivity
that once connected our bodies.

my mind drifts far away
from the body it once possessed
taking me places my
body cannot go
because it's in use.

the words *"round two"*
quickly snap me back to the body i once knew

the moment flies by for him
as he releases himself
into me.

anywhere but here

"Here, but not here"
were the words that slipped from between Your soft lips
when i asked You where Your feelings had gone.

what hurt me the most was
i was still there.

i felt every pull on my heartstrings
breaking out my chest
reaching to be reconnected
with the love i once knew.

the more our distance grew
i began to understand the words that crushed me
"Here, but not here."

that's what i felt with everyone who
wasn't You,
even those closest to me.

i was physically going through life
but mentally my thoughts were always
on You.

who were Your thoughts on when You were with me?
questions began to tug at my heart
requiring answers.

where did Your love go?
who did Your love go to?

the questions repeatedly pondered in my mind.

i went to You for comfort and peace
    but it was nowhere to be found.

my mind recalled
the love You once had for me
"to the moon and back"
You said.

i wept for
what once used to be
to the song
we once shared

the lyrics
cut deeper than ever before
oh how
 i miss those soft lips.

reminisce

is love the nervousness that i feel in my chest
when i see You?
or the smile that quickly crosses my face
when You hug me unexpectedly?

love,
what is love?

is love people leaving you without giving a reason?
or is it the goosebumps i feel on my skin whenever we are together?

will it still be love if it came from someone else?

i ask myself
is all affection good affection?
where i quickly answer with,
No!

it's Him!
it's His affection!
it's His love !
it's His love that fills the void in my heart
easing my overthinking...

it's His love
that wipes my tears away
when He tells me He loves me!

where i quickly answer with a question,
so much? i say
where He responds without pause
"So much..."

love is You,
love is what i feel
whenever i'm with You.

it's as simple as they weren't
You.

you
will come back

sob story

Your face is the only image that crosses my mind
when i close my eyes –

a sob story i tell myself...

i can't eat
i can't sleep
without You being with me –

a sob story i tell myself...

i dream of Us
in hopes that our connection rekindles
the pain that i feel in my chest
is a pain like no other
a pain that only love can bring –

a sob story that i tell myself...

is it love i want
or is it You i want –

a sob story i tell myself...

is it love that i need to find from within myself to be happy?
or is it You i need to be happy?

a sob story that i tell myself...

i cannot differentiate which one i need
when You're all i see
when You're all my mind rants about –

a sob story i tell myself...

a sob story i tell myself to make me feel better
but whenever i tell the story
tears flow out of my eyes
as if the pain is connected to the love i feel
whenever i think of You
it brings me back to the

sob story i tell myself...

i can't imagine not being by Your side
so how can You imagine not being by mine?

how effortlessly You forget about me
like our time together was a fantasy
that was only playing in my mind

a sob story on my end
but what is it on Yours
i ask myself?

i need Your attention –

> *no I need my attention*

i need Your love –

> *no I need to love me*

a sob story i tell myself...

a little whisper calls me out of my misery
and says "Love Yourself"

a sob story i tell myself...

Perfect Love

we all dream of love

a Perfect Love

a love like no other

an unconditional love

that loves on your worst day just as much as on your best day

the type of love that doesn't make you beg for all the little
things but is given with ease

a love that is reciprocated and doesn't leave you wondering if
the love is one-sided

the type of love that doesn't hold back secrets

the type of love that doesn't hide away when angry

but the love that shows through anger

the type of love that picks you up when you fall

calls you beautiful and handsome when you don't feel any of
that sort

we want a Perfect Love that is never fading and never failing

a love that will always be there for you

all along, it wasn't you that was needed

it was I

The Root

We Are Not Objects

We, as women
    Shouldn't be treated as objects.
We are tired of men treating us how kids treat
Their toys

They play with us for the moment
    And brag about pulling us
        Like we are prizes that were won

Once they have their fun
    They throw us away
        Like we are less than human

        They call us pretty
And tell us all the ways we are pleasing to their eyes
            And to their bodies

But what about what's pleasing to
    their souls?
        their hearts?
            their minds?

What I offer is way more than My beauty
And what's between My legs

     I ask questions like,
     Why do you like Me?
     And you say,
     "Because You're pretty"

     Ain't I more than what's on the outside?

     you act as if My beauty
          Is found in your compliments.
you look at all the ways I can please you sexually,
But what about the ways I can please you mentally?

Built on what?

A raw foundation
built on pure
    undisguised motives
something My past
    knew nothing about

All it knew was an
unstable foundation
held up by the
stakes of
    sexual desire
       and attraction.

How fleeting desire was
    that only kept us together for so long,

Until your eyes found the next person
               to analyze...
    And your lips found the next person
               to taste...
And your hands found the next person
               to touch...

Our foundation slipped between the cracks;
    it did not withstand the storms,
        the test of love.

Our desire to rip each other's clothes off
    didn't keep you home.

Yet with time
        the things that kept us together
no longer satisfied you enough
            to keep you from leaving.

No longer will the stakes
that hold My relationship up
be built on the fleeting desires
of the flesh

But the desires of **God**
will clothe us
in fine linen

God will be the stake that
hold us up:

>   Trust
>   Loyalty
>   Honesty
>   the footstools
>   on which we stand firm!

What wind can blow over,
>   what person can come against,
>>   when **God** is at the center?

The love that bonds us
>   will run deeper than the surface

This is something that My future
>   will know much of!

I am valuable

In the past,
I failed to see My worth
and that I was more than the flesh
that wrapped across My intellect

Now I know I deserve to be discovered
and admired for more than what
I look like on the outside

I had to see the worth that everyone
else lacked to see in Me
that I was important
even though others tried
to rid Me of confidence

Now I set My standards so high
that not even the tallest man can see
   he can no longer claim I'm easy to please
and all My goodies are for him to seize

No longer can anyone gain access
to My secret place

My
mind
body
and spirit
are the jewels of the sea
that deserve to be discovered
with time

I no longer put others' happiness before Mine
because I deserve happiness as well

I value the time **God** has given Me
and it is not to be played with
by things that no longer serve a purpose
in My life.

Beauty is everywhere,
But loyalty is rare.

i am who I am

No longer defined

I am a new creation in **Christ,**
the one that saved My weary soul.

I am not defined by the physical
     nor the temporary.

The things that I do not possess
     no longer wipe the smile from My face.

The world tries to speak to My gullible ears
and tell them the things they want to hear

As if
I am not beautiful as is!

As if
the clothes that are on My back
don't completely capture the style
that is unique to My identity!

The world says I'm not enough

As if

the creator of the universe

didn't sculpt Me perfectly to cultivate

the love and time

that **He** put in every shape and curve

to express the love that **He** has so deeply rooted in Me!

As if

the amount of money in My bank account

defines My worth and who I am!

Oh, how I

will no longer be defined by others

and held by the shackles of My feet

or directed down the path they think I should go

and the person they think I should be!

Who I Am

There's no longer a doubt of
        Who I Am!

I love the image I see
when I look in the mirror!

My heart skips a beat,
smiling at the fact
that it's experiencing a love
that once wasn't there!

Insecurities are no longer put on a pedestal,
defining Me!

I no longer focus on the beauty
that the outer can see,
but a beauty that runs deeply
in My bones and flesh
that have never known a love so great
puts a smile on My face

that can go on for miles
and miles!

I see **God** in Me,
filling every void
and taking away every doubt!

Who can take My joy away?

I am beautiful
And worthy of every good thing.

The aching

Split in two

have you ever been so scared to fall in love
that your heart shakes thinking of it?

uncontrollable tears emerge
from the depths of your soul
as the utter pain of being rejected by somebody
you love starts to arise in torment you

   remembering the heartbreak of your past
as your agonizing thoughts
       tell you the love
          won't be mutual

who will love you?
who can love you?

have you ever cried at the thought
  of experiencing another heartbreak?

oh, how love takes trust
the type of trust
  i no longer have to give

if there was a way i could build a brick wall around my heart
while loving you
i would

but loving you takes a part of me
                        that i no longer have to give
loving you opens me up to
pain
  rejection
          grief
so why would i choose that?

i'm faced with two options
walk away.
or stay.

i told myself i'd rather have a choice of how my pain hits me
i'd rather walk away
than to let it hit me out of nowhere.

i'm scared to lose Who I Am
in the face of Someone Else.

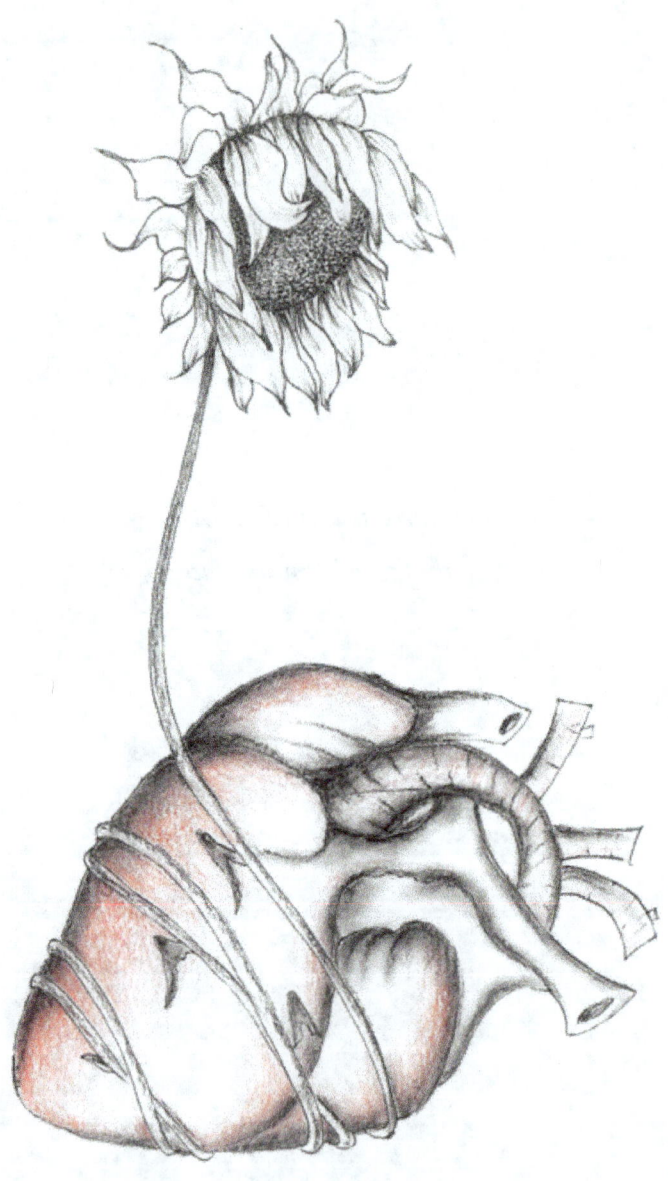

The Healing

who can hear? who can feel?

we search for love within the hearts of those who are broken –
hearts that have been abandoned
and kicked to the curb

hearts with wounds
unseen by the naked eye,
if the naked eye cannot see the wounds
then do they still exist?

a heart shattered into pieces
something that cannot be seen
but can be felt

as it pounds its last efforts to stay alive
as the pounds transmit the message
that the heart cries out
in an effort to be heard
by someone near

heal me, make me whole again

who can hear the heart cries?

what the heart wants
is what the heart gets, right?
but does the heart even know what it wants?

so, what happens when what the heart wants
it can't get?

it breaks,
it's tangible,
it locks itself up,
in efforts to never give someone that same love again.

you can't find love in my heart
there is no trust in my heart

and i can't love you
because my heart can't give you the love you need
because it's on its last pound
its last breath

it can't take another heartbreak

they say the last pound
is what draws the **Lord** near
the last pound
is the pound that the **Lord** feels

that breaks **His** heart
to see one of **His** loved ones broken

God can't be seen by the naked eye
but can be felt

as **He** draws close to the brokenhearted
and **His** love pours out
as **He** breathes life into the empty vessel

and whispers to the heart's silent cry of
heal me
and responds
"I Am,
I Am Here,
Be Free!"

solid ground

I anxiously await for the love of My life
to spring through the door,
longing for a love so intense,
it shoots chills straight up My spine,
declaring he's the one!

My heart was once bruised with past afflictions,
and covered with a smog that blinded it from recognizing love,
but now has been cleared away!

Now I recognize the one true love of all mankind –
the only person capable of giving the Perfect Love
that I desire!

Jesus Christ has placed My feet on solid ground
and passionately demonstrated
the true meaning of love!

The punishment is no longer
for Me to bear
and I am no longer trapped in a place of despair!

freed from My iniquities
and the bondage of My past,
through **Him** I am
renewed at last!

Dear Me,

I may not always see the beauty in Me
and My mind may replay the times I wish to forget,
but there will never come a time that I will hate Me
and discard the feelings of love again!

Not My strength but **His**!
Not My will but **His**!

I am more than what I thought
I could be!
and more than what I thought
I should be!

I thought what I experienced
was all there was to
love and life!

But the **Lord** has renewed My mind
and set Me free,
so I set My pride in **Him**,
and being made in **His** likeness!

I no longer carry the weight of burdens on My back
preventing Me from walking with My head held high!

Who can knock Me off My feet,
 when the **Lord** keeps Me stable?

Who can rage war in My mind,
when the **Lord** fights My battles?

Who can contaminate My emotions,
when the **Lord** guards the gates of My
soul?

My problems try to hold their ground
without knowing My **Lord** is bigger!

There is no place
and no room
for heartache and pain.

Do you know that My **Lord** is bigger than the sea
and all the problems that it brings?
But I am no longer scared of the problems that may come My way,
for My **God** will take Me by the hand
and guide Me through the wilderness.

As I sing **His** praises,
I'm confident that just as **He** has helped Me before,
He will more than happily help Me again!

People's love for Me was conditional,
*But **Jesus** loved Me unconditionally.*

The Let Go

Closure

I begged
and pleaded at the gateway
 of your heart.

   you shut Me out
   and drowned out My cries,
   not even My highest
   pitch could be heard.

A sudden shift
in our story
that I will never
quite grasp
of why I no longer
enticed you.

The closure that I
desperately sought will
never see the light of day,

but I can choose to close
this chapter,
the one that took
part of Me away.

A game of tug of war
we played
that was won by you,
you pulled with all your might against Me.
My heels clamped into the dirt
  as I dragged behind you,
begging you to stay.

  The rope began to leave
      bruises along My arms
        as I asked
          why?

But that answer was
not for you to give
but for Me to find within

My next chapter
  does not include you
and the loose parts that I tried
to hold close

your purpose was not to be with Me
    until the vows came screeching
      out of your mouth
    but you were simply a lesson
    that I will keep until the end of time

Now you fade off
    into the distance
 finding your purpose
apart from Mine

I won't hold on any longer
My hands are filled with blisters
 and I can feel My grip slowly loosen

But this time around
I will call this duel a tie
    Because now
        I Love Me
            in absence of you
                that's all the closure I need

This is not the end of My story
just the end of a chapter
we once shared
and the beginning of a
new life I now must live.

Mended

you weren't capable of giving Me a perfect love.
I let myself loose in you and you lost parts of Me
that I was left to find and put back together.

I thought love was over for Me
until I met a person named **Jesus**.

I am no longer afraid of what the tides may bring in.

No doubt runs freely in My mind
because I trust in the **Lord**
that **His** love will be the same
today,
tomorrow,
and
forever.

I laid Myself freely at **His** feet,

letting **Him** see all of Me

without shame or guilt,

and **He** accepted every part of Me

and loved every inch of Me,

even the parts that you could not love.

Oh, how unashamed I am to be loved by **Jesus**!

Be free

To the lovers of My past,
you are no longer held hostage in My mind,
but free to go.

Be free
and explore all there is to life
without Me.

I thought keeping the thoughts of you would keep Me safe
and provide Me with warmth and security.

But I was too hot to the touch,
burning all new lovers who tried to embrace My beauty,
leaving them with bruises and scars.
The guards I had around My heart
was a blazing fire,
burning all that came near.

I was a puppet in My mind
being swayed by My emotions,
but through poetry,
I freed Myself
from the puppeteer.

I no longer tense with fear
    or hide with shame.

I come naked before the world
    revealing the scars of My past.
They tell My story
and the stories of many others as well
so that we may all be free.

Confessions

In the beginning, it was you and me,
then i laid my sight upon You,
and suddenly there was a shift in my story.

It was no longer just my story but our story.
all my i's and me's became Us's and we's,
and together we became inseparable.

Now it's just Me,
then there's you –
another scar that needs healing.

you arose in My darkest moments
like a candle that lit the way –
you showed the way, but your feet led Me
to My grave, and I was too blinded to see.

The story of us ends
but another must begin...

There is more pain in holding on
Than letting go.

A New Beginning

Dear Love,

Oh love,
I'm ready to fully embrace every good thing
that comes with you.

Although it was a journey to get to this point,
I will never retrace My steps.
you taught Me things about Myself
and revealed to Me the good and the bad.

I no longer need him to be happy
or rub My feet
or tell Me how beautiful I am.

When I look in the mirror,
the words come praising out of My lips.

I no longer need
his attention or his love,
Because the love I found wraps Me up at night.
it kisses Me good night
and reminds Me of how proud they are of Me
on how far I have come.

My mind no longer echoes the cruel thoughts
that I used to think of Myself
but now sings My praises.

Oh love,
how you changed Me,

I no longer let My peace be disrupted
nor let others speak death to My soul.

I found a beauty that cannot be torn from Me
by the constant changes of the world.

My beauty runs deeper than the eyes can see
and the hands can touch,
deeper than the outer shell of My heart
that was once lifeless,
deeper than My lungs
that breathe life into My soul.

I am ready to dive headfirst into the
ocean of wonders
where there's much more to be
 explored!

To have and to hold — Me

Till Death Do Me Part
 I whispered
As I set a flame to the rope
Of what once used to be

My happiness is no longer boasted
For the world to see
   My lips no longer
   Shout and scream
   For those near to hear

Once submerged in complete darkness,
I finally took a breath
And breathed in the true meaning of life

Pain no longer has its filthy claws on Me
Get back, I say!
Because now I can see the light of day

The lover of My past no longer sustains My life
My happiness is no longer intertwined
With his love

I can love Me and let go of his hands too

  The love I have is sacred
And not for the whole world to seize

The **Lord** gave Me beauty for My ashes
  And joy for My sadness

Once taken from dirt and made into Me
To dirt I will go back peacefully

But until then, I will love Me wholeheartedly
And I will never find My worth in those I lay eyes on
Because My **God** up above has already declared Me worthy
Of every good thing

But until **God** parts the sky and the angels
  Come singing My name
Till Death Do Me Part

I will shout

    And scream

Until My vocal cords can no longer contain the words

I have to say

But until then the whole world will know

How finally I let go.

To be continued...

Dear Reader

First, it's pain

But know in the beginning,
letting go will hurt.

You will pour out
every last tear until your eyes dry out.

Air will be drawn from your lungs,
causing your breathing to become choppy.

Every sound that gives voice to your pain
will become silent.

You may begin to eat very little,
disappearing from those who love you
in the dark corners of your mind,
while letting depression overtake you.

But steadfast, knowing
storms will come,
striking down every little thing you own,
leaving a mess that seems irreversible.

But after every storm,
the sun must shine,
restoring all the flowers.

You are the flower!

I encourage you to look towards brighter days
that will begin to draw you up.

Remember, you are not alone on your journey.
Learn to love yourself with an unconditional love
and never let love part.

Invaluable

If you ever been told you weren't enough,
know in God's eyes
you are more than enough!

God sees what others lack to see in you!
where people see imperfection,
God sees true perfection!

God sees your heart
and understands things that no one else can understand!
God sees your tears
and He works in your favor!

Keep your head up
and do not let their hurtful words get to you.

You got this!
You are worthy!
You are enough!